GRACE SHIVER

ALSO BY CATHY STONEHOUSE
POETRY
The Words I Know

FICTION
Something About the Animal

NON-FICTION
Double Lives: Writing and Motherhood
(with Shannon Cowan and Fiona Tinwei Lam)

GRACE SHIVER

poems by

Cathy Stonehouse

inanna poetry & fiction series

INANNA Publications and Education Inc.
Toronto, Canada

Canada Council   Conseil des Arts
for the Arts   du Canada

 ONTARIO ARTS COUNCIL
CONSEIL DES ARTS DE L'ONTARIO

The publisher gratefully acknowledges the support of the Canada Council for the Arts and the Ontario Arts Council for its publishing program.

The publisher is also grateful for the kind support received from an Anonymous Fund at The Calgary Foundation.

Cover design: Val Fullard
Interior design: Luciana Ricciutelli

Library and Archives Canada Cataloguing in Publication

Stonehouse, Cathy
    Grace shiver : poems / by Cathy Stonehouse.

(Inanna poetry & fiction series)
ISBN 978-1-926708-23-2

    I. Title. II. Series: Inanna poetry and fiction series

PS8587.T674G73 2011   C811'.54   C2011-906163-5

Printed and bound in Canada

Inanna Publications and Education Inc.
210 Founders College, York University
4700 Keele Street
Toronto, Ontario M3J 1P3 Canada
Telephone: (416) 736-5356 Fax (416) 736-5765
Email: inanna@yorku.ca Website: www.yorku.ca/inanna

In memory of M. *&* G.

Contents

*What is spoken is never, and in no
language, what is said.*
—Martin Heidegger

I.
Without the Bodies Necessary to Fill it …

Thursday Morning in the Peace Museum

I.
Skin hangs off these orphaned children like rags. Behind them a red
lamp gutters before a charcoal-rendered backdrop of imagined pain.
In a tall glass case, charred fingernails and melted bone fragments,
the checkered remnants of a fifty-year-old kimono whose black
bamboo stripes melted into its wearer's back; the rust-wrapped
tricycle of a two-year-old boy who was killed instantly by the blast,
now buried by his parents beside him; the bubbled surfaces of melted
roof tiles, the buckled sides of green glass sake bottles, a bodhisattva
with a melted face.

The disappeared do not pass away. The baby who suckled for milk
at its dead mother's breasts never left our sight, the woman burnt to
a cinder where she stood, one leg still lifted, her monumental effort
to escape become a photographic negative branded into the corneas
of those who saw yet survived.

Death is always happening. Sometimes a person just has to close
their eyes.

3

II.
When I looked up from my sweet potato garden
A fireball exploded like a red-hot poker flower in the sky.
It had been a completely cloudless, sunny morning, hot enough to
sweat just standing still. In the stillness about the Inland Sea, the
exact, unhurried positioning of the American B29 bomber the
Enola Gay was approximately 12,000 metres above sea level.
Did its pilot take his bearings from the sun?
The temperature beneath the epicenter is estimated to have risen
as high as 6,000°C.
In the *ryokan* I pass a German couple in the hallway. We nod at
each other reluctantly, open our separate doors with jangling keys.
In my four-mat room a ripe banana waits, along with fresh hot water
for my tea. As I open my giant bamboo-wrapped *onigiri* I imagine
the children who picked live maggots out of their raw burned sides,
mistook them for giant rice grains, the darkness that fell across
their eyes.
Until the A bomb fell, Hiroshima remained relatively untouched.
It was considered necessary by the U.S. government —
It was considered necessary.
An early plum rain courses down my outside walls. In this room
without windows I don't know if it's night or day, Japan or Canada.
I can read all the facts but some of the heat just can't penetrate, the
cracked glass on top of the piano, the economic miracle of melted
bodies
Melted bodies
From which the disappeared do not pass away.

III.

Christmas Day in Tokyo is a pale nativity without the birth. Two
lifelike plastic mannequins of toddlers stare into a lighted sweet shop
window, dressed in scarves and hats, while blond-haired blue-eyed
cherubs sing the praises of frosted glass ornaments, fir trees, sleigh
bells, marzipan, off key, and in the centre of the plastic stable God's
crib is empty; each Buddha's long since reached enlightenment and
moved on.

Tokyo: sign of perseverance,

Sack upon sack of origami cranes; at the children's peace memorial, a
dark snake of schoolboys in high-necked Prussian uniforms unravels
into awkward jokes, despair.

Sadako Sasaki folded six hundred and forty-four paper cranes; Jun
Hase was decapitated by his eleven-year-old schoolmate. In the wake
of war all freedom bears the flag of loneliness.

When we cannot imagine hell we make it.

Oh when will the bells of New Year start to sound?

5

IV.

Just for a moment I find I have to close my eyes.

I have stared down this concrete tunnel shaped like an
old-fashioned North American settlers' wagon toward a peace
flame that never yet went out until my eyes blurred, I have traced
the silvered feathers of the mourning doves at liberty amongst the
cenotaphs until their softness vanished with the light, then like a
burn victim seeking salve for my fingers I have buried my hands in
the smooth yet jagged rainbows of traditional Japanese folded paper
cranes, I have wondered about the old women dressed in overalls
and cotton bonnets who sweep up the peace park's litter, about the
fallen cherry blossoms and shriveled camellia petals that gather like
shucked-off human skin cells along the footpaths between
manicured lawns, have wondered about the middle-aged
brain-damaged children of the *hibakusha* who wear their socks and
turtlenecks pulled up tight, hold onto their aged mothers' hands as
the streetcar they ride passes *Genbaku Domu*, Atomic Bomb Dome,
and who carry their bodies tenderly, accusingly as if their feet were
silenced copper gongs.

I have stared down the eyes of the Kannon of Chugu-ji Temple,
her averted gaze has driven me further in. I have stared at myself in
the mirror above the rust-stained sink next to the public bath in the
ryokan hidden behind leaves in the deserted rain-bright streets of
Kyobashi-cho. I have washed the marble statuettes of Jizo lined
up beneath gold-leaf lanterns in the quiet of the Universally
Illuminating Cave, have lifted each long long-handled silver ladle
that rested in the sweet wet of a well. I have sat for hours in silence
on the soft give of tatami and not sought enlightenment, knelt

before the giant Buddha of Nara and not asked forgiveness, only
tempted to curl up and sleep in his twelve-foot hand.

I have wanted for nothing, and yet I have wanted to die here.
Like the sweet smell of jasmine and incense, of thousand-year-old
skin dust scattered over ancient bamboo scrolls, like the work parties
of half-starved children who looked up at the sky and saw a flash
that distant morning in August of the nineteenth year of the
Showa era, I have wanted to be buried immediately forever in a
dark tomb of undiscoverable non-witness before the glare of summer
shrivels God.

V.

Between the instant in which the bomb began to fall
And the instant in which the bomb had already fallen, seventy
thousand memories burned out;
During the soft explosion of ink onto paper there can be no
stopping such a thought.
Despite his age the old *hibakusha* tonsured like a monk still bleeds
calligraphy; at the souvenir stall spills its grace across visitors'
outstretched notebooks, accepts coins from their bamboo-coloured
hands. The ink stick he uses is solid, fist-sized, traditional, its
ingredient simple: the dried black soot of pine resin. As he rubs its
worn edge back and forth across a wetted ink stone, what thickens
is a soft black pool of burns; his wife's decapitated body

Which flickers before his eyes like a premonition every time he
smiles, then his own pocked and irradiated torso, so slow in dying,
and their demolished wood and paper family home

When I take up the harp
All at once my grief breaks forth

VI.

In the peace museum each sharp intake of breath is a measurable event. Wheelchairs and walking sticks catch on the varnished edges of communicating doors. A troop of young boys from Vernon, BC skip to and fro between models of downtown Hiroshima before and after the thermonuclear blast. A man in split-toed work boots whispers sutras. *Did you see the pickled stomachs? Cool. Far out.*

The human shadow, once imprinted on the steps at the entrance to the Sumimoto Bank at Kamiya-cho 250 metres from the hypocenter draped itself across a temple wall. Its tattered width marks out the distance between a miracle and a holocaust.

In Hiroshima-jo I climb steep wooden stairs up to a look out. Steel office buildings, pillars of white smoke: captains of industry stare back from every side. In the dark of the afternoon, history vanishes softly from black lacquered armour upright without the bodies necessary to fill it, from sword blades polished until they are smiles made up of water that rest their brightness on a black silk dais. Down on the third floor a holographic tour guide explains the castle's wooden fortification, why samurai warriors are like sakura. Meanwhile children flower.

Questionnaire

I.
So you think you are:
a) free b) physically imprisoned
c) psychologically and emotionally entangled
d) all, none or part of the above
But who did you kill after you finished your coffee?
Whom did you find yourself crushing between your heels?
Take a look; I know it's hard. See where they leashed us.
Are you a woman undressed, a toxic substance,
your biography an accumulation of surrendered privileges that
over time acquires stains,
your ancient brain pickled in peat, the source of all the latest
celebrity gossip?
Or are you leisure, entertainment?
Somewhere in this house is an illegal alien. Somewhere in this
room a hate-crime occurred.

[handwritten annotations: "Burn email.", "—rhetorical? If so, what is it?", "maybe saying you don't know...?", "implied? rhetorical?", "—Standards? social", "opposite?", "at which", "bog bodies", "—re ferring to a,b,c,d at beginning", "rebellion? not fitting in", "poverty? doesn't fit in with society"]

10

II.

What do you remember of your time there? I mean the refugee camp,
which wasn't just a way station. The language of symptom
so valuable: without it nothing but sleep, ornamental gesture.
Did you say what you meant? Dear Christ, he was my very first
prisoner: a cache of cold knives, a watch with the face of a saint.
You call this pessimism. Well watch me sink, bob up, present a new
populist contour while you starve and are reborn as a Dora re-run.
The man in the chicken suit; abortive food drops. Black plastic
pulled across the sun. As a child I lay awake, the night a terrifying
prospect, evidence of crime I was desperate to protect myself from.
Now when you slide I catch and surrender, relieved and inchoate,
my child self still oscillating, curving the fabric of time until it bends
backwards, my eyes raw wounds legislated to shine forever without
Diego ever breaking through.

Killing living backers?

III.

The woman is plain; the woman is not very attractive. She has grey hair, dark skin, no breasts, an excess of untreated blemishes. She is over 45, under 2, clinically insane and severely disabled. She could use a Brazilian. The woman is a great singer but asymmetric. She has no hands, no money and too many theories. She could use a haircut. She could use Internet access. Her pants are made of mud and her shoes of rubber. She delights in mismatched accessories, crutches and hearing aids, wears Wal-Mart to work and Versace to die in. She is cutting edge. She has too many teeth, a dead son and a toxic liver, an idea of beauty that involves the destruction of property, urgent peace talks and a reliable source of clean water. The woman is dying. The woman is a Head of State. The only remaining speaker of an indigenous language, she has no nationality and fallen arches. She is undernourished, obese and grief-stricken, a foxy redhead, dumb blonde, undistinguished brunette. In her previous appearance on-screen she was being gang-raped. Her extensive scarring renders her disturbing to look at. Nevertheless we applaud her courage, her chutzpah, and hope she makes it through to the Finals alive.

Fragments for Mothers

I.

Snowstorms in Beijing, drought in Manila
Death's weather different according to dialect
Unfurl the flag, the shredded lyric

Brown bear, brown bear, what do you see?

Soldier boys with muscular buttocks
Thumbs on each console, shooting down heretics

[handwritten annotations:] death is not equal, minorities, location, war ... also dialect more metaphorically (nurture) situation

contrast - children - innocence - war ... very effective.

peoples disobeying beliefs

not even bad people necessarily just like the boys. So...

[handwritten at bottom:] 1. Your child will not be to

II.

Do not take my glue. I need it to speak with. Decorate these walls
with pictures of castles, the skin of tomorrow already pricked and
moist.

mother/babies *foreshadow of the death*

Milk seeps. I am a king but rule over jam tarts only. Pieces of enrage
interleaved with stroke: your crown, my death-blow. What is it we
are? Today the snow is bright, my mouth a bird's beak, open to soft
hatfuls of buffoonery.

interleaved with tracing paper? *consolation/condense* *but*

elude *lo ssssrsin e* *relevant*

Hair is lewd. He will wash his hands in the body electric now refuge
from contempt is no longer pertinent. Most walks take longer than
expected. I calm myself by ensuring my tent flaps are fastened.

? vagina?

soil? *sound pronounced with expiration of breath* *dies*

A letter "F," half aspirate, retreats into a cupboard to fondle satin as
the ground beneath it changes, stays constant. Crawl in right now.
Here, into my reconditioned uterus. Shit stinks and love is fungible,
dear.

pin *try again* *Fact #1* *mutually interchangeable* *fact... #2?*

*2. The world needs fixing —
it is dangerous*

14

III.

insubstantial arine —

Little chocolate hearts tucked beneath bandages in the doll hospital:
Nina Simone sang of lynching with tenderness, as if the noose could
be dissolved
By her voice; in fifty years there will be no boreal forest:
Where will North be then? Sulfuric Eros

many issues — too many, slavery, you aren't everything

pretty, promising
I had a little palm tree, nothing would it bear
But a silver bullet and a shell-shocked stare
our ideals

A tisket, a tasket, your head falls in my basket/
Explosives strapped to genitals, all this in miniature —
Dear Christ, Mohammed of the burned hour

line break? why? or is it an alternative P.O.V.

destroying human ability to reproduce. Self-destruction

3. *our ideals lead to destruction, because destruction is inevitable, And human fault.*

15

IV.

Snowdrops beside the hedge flower while you lie in hospital
        Thank you thank you to all the bees in the world for your
wonderful honey
Death slides sentences into a silver envelope; a shard of blue
porcelain

Calls your aorta delinquent, in crisis less than war yet more than
concussion
        Pushing prognoses along as if immortal
Closed wounds, yellow/ purple, found beside salt in a
pollen-saturated landscape
        Can you move if you're killed, can you answer your
mother's questions

Reasons for genocide: this is how spring comes
Witness this planet's decrepitude, piling up mad riches of hot wax

V.

Pink and purple glitter, fluff saturation,
Reality a pipe bomb, bipolar stealth avatar
So listen, do not act.
I'd forgotten how far away news really takes us —
Out into the crude blue Paleolithic
Where Gwyneth Paltrow crunches up electronically
And no one asks if bliss is black or white.
Excuse me, children. Your parents have just been informed
[In distressing parentheses]
And the actual smoothly abducted. All minutes lost.
And yes, my son is a genius. He walked before he was born.
Bombs dropped on believers. Revelations
In the so-called "parrot position." Internal organs
Spilling into one's crib at night
As if the self were divided,
And as if not

When should the reveal occur?

VI.

Why are parents bad?
Because children need them

Because they are adults
And we can never forgive them
For letting the side down

reality.
Shattering illusion of
innocence.
Loss of innocence

Where the ghosts have been hiding all day

always have been
there.

(cannot forgive b/c they lied)

18

II.
Wake …

slipped heaven I

lost my body   armless statue
devolved into a hundred tongued sense nations

***

~~speared~~
baby lip
burst vaginal coinage

~~split~~
moon despot
snagged on the horn of symptom

***

retinude of tiny laid-back stars

slow , broke
pathology of witness
averted syntax
stroke
comprehension)
no milk left in these dumb breasts
) incest whores

the unsayable : crutchlike
plated with gold
derision or epidural

proof against kindness
honey that does not destroy

bargaining with wooden
entryways of trust
the eye the esophagus the authentic
DNA of infant demons

nonbeing's fascia
iridescent with human bliss-lusts

holy child , do not swim
to be small
is not a contraceptive

suicide
hope : law's
boneless knife
cuts away at face
frail neuroleptic :
tend me while I turn aside my faith

I know murderers
they are not black but white

paper sperm
ensuring minute
social rips

night-light
knife-wiped

~~blood~~
is not contagious silence
mother

take the long view
grief that is not expressed
suffocates future beings

do you understand why you are here

dark integer
stepping through the lock
you cure lucidity
detach retinas of fire
to voyage mentallic , heart-soaked
into the unmedicated beyond

strapped to her cradleboard
unlyred tomorrow doctor

don't drink blood unless it is a toast

I birthed oblivion
it was a small soul

sharp-toothed animal brain
softened with lenses

nest that lived
unruptured by heat song

wants to assimilate?

fathers , dresses , gods

what do you wish for?

grammar:
blood transit spasm

do you believe
contracted
into birdvoice

iron
opened
mouth

the chill of
red harm , leaving

epileptic with scarring
no anal sphincter
to speak of

love
in this context
is paradise
wrapped in a shroud

grace shiver

where is swaddled safety
but the axis

---

a beloved's ribs
circled by compass needles

hold my feet oh god
grease me with rest
night lice
a scuttled warship's armour

navel of tender slaughter

touched by the hem of light
oh kissed, lost one

let me breathe
your breached sensorium
in scission

---

aurora'd precipice

fall
into your thousand-saddled wake

III.
A Child's Prayer …

Now the day is over, night is drawing nigh

The child sleeps in soldier pajamas. All night they march across her yet stay still: blue cotton infantry who press out from the threadbare fabric, red flannel muskets that rise up from her body like a rash. In the afternoons this room is bright yet cool, its scratched-up bunk beds glitter with a storm cloud's sheen; at night she props the bedroom door ajar, watches pools of watery dark seep through. An hour ago she prayed for Mum and Dad, for her aunts, uncles, cousins and grandmothers, for her brother who sleeps in the bunk above, for the slats of steel that hold him there and for the pale blue cover of the Children's Prayer Book, for its simple, bloodless skin of heavenly light. Now she presses lifelined palms together, prays for the simple fact of infinite space and as floorboards creak and hands tick out their circuits remembers again the blank face of the ghost — *when it sits by me please don't let it touch me, and please let me please let me remember, please let me remember its face*.

Shadows of the evening steal across the sky

She cannot forget the mossy teeth of death that rise up in the guise
of children's graves: *July 8th 1861 – November 14th 1862: Fly Back
Home To Jesus Blessed Dove*: the answers to such marble slates of
sums are scrawled across the damp backs of her hands. *Jesus wants
me for a sunbeam, to shine for him each day!* The night wind stirs then
quells its choir of beech leaves, opens up their flat lips to the rain.
Even the words to children's hymns spell out secrets called out by
the dead, while sleep has become a Neolithic cave, a dark amphora,
so unlike a solid bedroom door. Delicate as brim-full china jugs, she
lifts her ghostly feet across its threshold, careful not to break each
glass meniscus, shatter terror's brittle, rigid mouth.

Comfort every sufferer watching late in pain

She peels up out of child-skin like a genie, watches her bottle-body
gently glow. Her tongue is a magic flying carpet from which she
unwraps spangled minarets, presses them into the night sky like
spring bulbs then dreams she is a small boy on a raft with a sea-slug
penis that stirs green phosphorescence through starred dark while
through the air black centuries, burnt Bible pages mingle, blown
past by dreamers whose wistful breath she meets then rises on. She
dreams and dreams then wakes up in the carapace of self, trapped
against its wingless polished back, dresses herself with velvet,
sleep-gloved hands. Through the dark the click of suitcase locks
has now unsnapped her body from her head: beside the window her
daddy stands against a full moon's light, shadow rubbed into his skin,
alternate face placed inside a Co-op carrier bag. His black coat's
finely hand-sewn folds tremble with a short storm's minute thunder,
as the ceremonial skins of ancestors are smoothed down. She wants
to place her feet upon his shoes, yet her night-time body is poised
above chthonic oceans; its descent curves deeper than a cormorant's
dive. As the family gathers up its vastness, carries sorrow down the
rain-slick path, the bodies of archangels implode softly while the
blackboards of B-roads are printed across by chalk white faces, their
terrible tonnage of stored grief.

Those who plan some evil from their sin restrain

She sits within an ash-marked circle caresses flagstones as if they
were her best friend's hands Candles' blades, unsheathed around
the room cast their shuddering light across masked faces threaten
to shake solidity from her grasp   yet what could be more real than
eager tongues, embittered by the taste of swallowed fear What
could be more real than a twelve-year-old boy who holds a
scythe-shaped knife up to his chest Here in the night adults groan
and touch their private selves those small pink spaces where
untruths begin   while children are instructed to dance they
must turn spirals in a leftward circle mark minutes with their
depthless stride   as the young ones lift up hands from frozen torsos
their adults unleash tongues and tighten fists and only the mangled
Real trapped inside bodies can't wake up though its language says
it's time   As sound and fingers reach up high a subtle music spins
out toward morning rabbit screeches faces burnt by purple ropes
of blood and what is it that she can never say That she dreams of
bread and milk while muscle falters that death is a golden cymbal
crashed then blessed

Through the long night watches may thine angels spread

It wasn't she who died; yet she is numb and lifeless to the touch, pinches her own skin hard, twists each wrist until it mottles pink. Scraps of cloud push through thinning darkness while thrushes, bullfinches gather on the staves of telegraph wires, ready to announce a blue-glass day. Here, within her church-of-all-the-worlds, she feels her season tip toward the dark, its ice close up across her face, touches the blurred discs of bruises that blood will never blossom through, undo. Angry spirits claw her hair, rub their dry words along her tongue until trees along the brightening road come clear, their bronze-leaved, blood-berried trunks shimmer, slick with sloes, hips, insects, *life*, and she settles back into her bed-time body; a long cold winter has begun.

Their white wings above me, watching round my bed

Her mother pats cool talc between warm toes, abrades her daughter's chest with towels that smell of peaches, cinnamon, washing-up liquid, hot toast. It's Sunday, and the coloured blocks of school-days press up bright against the window glass. Damnyou damnyou damnyou damnyou — only her mother's soap-cracked, blue-veined fingers can smooth away such curses from soft lips, only her Mummy can wash away bad words, cure upset tummies, stitch up dollies' strained, unravelled seams, close wounds that throb until fear dissipates, would leave half a sleeping pill placed by her daughter's bed: Take it, it'll do you good. The child accepts such cool white presences now that daytime's light has come and gone, now that folded newspapers, mugs of tea and tiddly-wink board-game tokens have faded into mocking, egglike shapes; for night returns, and she has nothing left to suck or hold, only the polished face of daytime Mummy who unpacks the skulls of smaller, scarier Mummies; smiling, hollow, endlessly recessed.

IV.
Fugue Trimester ...

Fugue Trimester

The red book you are written in is gone. An apple from the
highest branch, my pregnancy with you once filled me with longing,
provoked in me an urge to climb ladders, trust my entire weight to
fences of air.

The sun slants your voice into my mailbox. No one else hears it.

Grace within grief falls, angel vertiginous.
A short white casket
filled with black flowers. Tufted blanket stitched from bone and ash.

Dead girl —
Facts are so small. None of yours have ever been delivered.

Once, in the little hollow before waking, I felt your warm fingers
at the back of my neck. Perhaps there was a kiss, too, muscular as
voles' feet. A slowly-crumbling statue of deliberation, as I wondered
whether to turn on your future's light.

ca

Nothing is as uneven as the weather. One moment it is blue
morning, the next thing we know the world is at war.

My border disappears just as your shadowed hand reaches forward.
I watch it fall through an opening the size of your face.

I'd give up speech just to watch your sealed eyes open. But the prayer
wheels of winged seeds conspire against us, dry veined syllables
twinned at the root.

જ

Loud reports of indignities at dusk.
Dark seeps out through libraries of unfinished drafts.
Perhaps after a year you will become oak sap, thin enough to bleed
through veins of leaves.

In dream I hang verbs high, where the wind might catch them.

Last night I discovered thirteen blue wolf cubs, curled helplessly on
their backs in snow. Some had dried-out eye sockets. Still, I scattered
lavender over their smallness. I knew, like ideas for books, some
would survive.

છ

Sometimes what is dead appears newborn, while what has just been born appears to have died: A fungal growth; the supple leather coats of the newly promoted; the intricate nervous systems of umbrellas, trees.

Dried violet stem each night I touch you, hope in perpetuity, white-bitten grass.

ℂℝ

Who doesn't feel the rain of the heart: a sentimental wash of
celadon blue? Your body on a trolley ready for shipping. The blood
of a bird smeared across the sidewalk. As dark comes on, I realize I
am too late.

Soldiers mourn lost legs, irreplaceable faces. Skin is a form of death.
No war has ended. The hospital where you bled out, a spirit gateway,
torn down and replaced by the open road.

❧

My *left leg is imprisoned,* read my manifesto: *because men in polished shoes have declined to free it.*

While you slept, I discovered an abandoned typewriter at a city bus stop. An unfinished letter to you, my lost limb, still inside it. Two silver keys entangled above the letter 'b'.

Used to exist? or never was even formed?

&

If pretending you hadn't lived helped, I would have tried it. Instead I express milk, swab ghost incisions. Your mouth latched onto my nipple, an incomplete thought. *never happened*

 # write piece
architecture?

છ

When the storm finally hits, I spill medication all over the bed-
clothes: cartridges of ink, all water soluble. In the morning create
an animal out of my own blood. Snow settles on your forehead. You
cannot breathe yet. In my sheets discover theories of unwashed hair.
Brain cells lived in like bunk beds, where banned thoughts sleep
alternate eight-hour shifts.

(paint me, wash me, in confusion)

There's a blind religious faith at work in resemblance, like a sword
in its sheath or a woman with her eyes half-open, feeling a way back
out along scars.

જ

What I need most right now is the scent of jasmine. Any small won-
der that tells me your face is still here. I wish that you could tell me
about the future, where milk will come from when there's no grass
left. Do you remember the alarm clock that flowered last Novem-
ber? Snow on sweat, your birth into a hospital toilet. Such timeless
mischief tender to God's tongue.

ଔ

When your parachute dropped I felt my body harden, become a shell
whose lips were made of bone. I reached for pain like a handle whose
trapdoor might open. Behind it were stiff garments of guilt, dissent.
But the window onto that garden was no longer there. A bowl fell,
my veins collapsed, and fever started building its irreversible etching
up sorrow's peak.

Disaster appears beautiful in winter's half-light.
Like the cold hands of the actual, a schism sculpted by dogs,
or energy's next wife –
a blue hand leads it past feeling, thinking
                              into the bed of whatever god governs beyond.

Teleogram

TATTOO NEEDLES FINE SILVER HYPODERMIC WIRES
JET INTO AN INFANT'S NERVE-ENDS THE FINE SKIN
OF BABY FINGERNAILS AN ELECTRICITY AS BLUE AS EYELIDS
THAT RIFLES THROUGH HISTORICAL ERAS RENDERS PAIN AN
EXQUISITE HALO OF ONTOLOGICAL GRACE

UNDERNEATH THIS BLACK X-RAY OF UNDISTURBED
BRIGHT BONES ARE VEINS AND ARTERIES THAT FOOLISHLY
PUMP SALT BLOOD AGAINST ALL ODDS STOP THE CHILDREN THE
CHILDREN WHERE ARE THE CHILDREN THEIR FINGERS TRANSLATE
TRUST AND AMNESTY OUT OF PAPER BODIES SUCH AS THESE

Another Little Flower for God's Garden

ᥫ

please god please don't hurt me can I
tell you summat I must tell you summat please
mum I cannot tell you I cannot breathe

CR

Myra
photographed with the dog, Puppet
on the very graves of the lost: their bodies pressed
into acid peat beneath her two-inch heels   Dave Smith
who finally called the police
about Ian Brady — I didn't think he was cracked I thought he was
intellectual
I thought he was impressive his philosophy about Jews and pornogra-
phy seemed right —
pictured with his wife and daughter
ten years after the last axe fell
one child in winter, one child in summer:
such flowers planted beneath the moor
do not flourish   beautiful yet unrepeatable, their names
form crystals inside the mouths of journalists, hangers-on:
Pauline, Edward, Keith, Lesley Ann and John

જી

this is the nightmare sound   of a woman calling
it might be from the past   it has that quality
the broken courage   of the constantly bereft

her name   a character
which stands for exiled from history
a verb   which translates as to abandon hope

and this the airless sound   of someone
falling
the freighted dissonance   of a spirit   come to rest

for this is the secret room where shots are practiced
the notebook of truth
sent overboard   with the rest

and this an infant body being broken
by the distant   punctual   horror
of the ritually   obsessed

for this is the nightmare sound
of a woman drowning   her face
sheeted with tears

her body ·   wrestling

who might be drowning now   she has that quality
the ink-smeared authenticity
of the not-yet-   photographed

the blue-   black lungs
      of the silenced
      the dispossessed — no spirit

ଔ

a giant Clydesdale that slipped and lay on cobbles panting
Ian Brady took it as a sign that death would follow him always
from the Glasgow slum into the insurance office up up
onto the sheer naked chest the empty brown scrub
of Saddleworth Moor
he took it and carried it within him as every child does in
desperate circumstances but how it transmogrified into a cult
of numb nazi lips the Nuremberg speeches the ax that came
down onto the last one's head the mess on Granny Maybury's
living room door no one knows, the experts of the criminal
justice system tell the grieving mothers, no one knows
oh the green face of death that rises up and calls on him

୧

only now the mothers re-appear
vacuuming up crisp crumbs   tail-ends of skate
knocked off the kiddies' plastic plates —
they pull up our school socks   straighten our
striped school ties   chase us daily, relentlessly out of
     bedclothes —
these mothers we forget to kiss and hug
mothers of convicted murderers   mothers of forgotten murdered
     ones

V.
A Scar ...

After the massacre

there was no room left
                              inside
to describe nerve cells,
the fire of anesthesia
burning up loose bones,

there were no words
                              disconnected
from the skin
of the severing blade:

after the massacre
there were no words:

                    words
had lost their shells,   crawled
          naked about the floor
          severed, bleeding

                    even his body
looped,   curved
          across the torture table

visual image. Bea-full.

like a wide question mark:

?

after the massacre
there were no

words.

*but still thoughts,
wondering
why?
a whole conundrum!
there's always
more!*

(after the massacre)

it was necessary to
                          turn my head
it was necessary not to
                          bleed

it was necessary to make notes
on the insides of my fingers
with the nib of a broken pen

it was necessary

it was all quite necessary

(to forget)

even the skull fragments
the baby's fingernails
the lock on the church basement door
that led down to the
screaming of children,

of night cats
in hallucinogenic air —

it was necessary

it was all quite necessary

after the massacre
I died again

this time in my own language

a silent sculpture
moulding the skin on my face
into a new mask
rupturing it, a scar
across constant movement:

never any time to rest -

hamstring snapped
shoulder blade broken
eye pulled out
or finger bone taken

then the scent of death, the stench
of sweat and burnt
skin, dying

on the cusp of midnight

79

and

no answer,

never any answer.

after the massacre I fell
a thousand times lower than the sun

I lost my ribs
in the darkness

no one was left to
speak or touch
except the shells
we had kept waiting
by the door:
we put them on.

we carried
our smoking chimneys
our horse flesh rank with sweat from the battlefield

our silences

over the ledge
to face morning:

after the massacre

there was frost
                    sweet as oranges
there was gravity
and sound

there was no mess left
(there were boxes)

there was nothing
(a clean dress for tomorrow)

there were pages

there was something
new as cinders
in the smell of my father's hands

VI.
What Remains …

The One who Left

He who could have been perfect, how he mocks you
Perfected as he was, now buried, lost
Thief who carried close your vital statistics
Incubus who stole your fate and ran

Supposed to love him, miss him, you despise him
Little biter, screamer in the pram
How he got inside you none can reckon
Shadow-brother, beast without a heart

New blood mixed with old a tragic potion
Features pressed up tight, defining yours
Foul mouth swallowing whole his sudden absence
You think you can disguise his mortal thoughts

Yet see these marks ...
These are signs of his progress
He whose place you held in the book of the living
He who held your place in the book of death

When a Picture Falls Somebody Dies

I remember the day my father's picture fell:
African violets trimmed by a gilt-edged frame,
its elastic band crumpled into boneless fingers,
my stilled heart greeting its thud.
It was then I heard the massing horses,
muscled chests locked inside the face of the clock.
My brother said he could hear them —
when he placed his ear to the pillow
each night, the roaring would start.
Sometimes, falling asleep, he even saw them,
all in a twisting string
a red fall down into death I could hear his
bed shake, feet slam as he met the ground
upright
to keep the luck in, like the horseshoe
our father kept above the door.

We knew that they lived in the loft:
its white sliding board edged with cracks
pulled back above our heads
to a place where only fathers go;
yet we must never name them, never quite see
the faces that spat up suddenly
before we had a chance to stop them,
after we had placed our shoes on a table
or opened an umbrella inside.

For they galloped quietly along unseen roads,
flashing inside the knife drawer, leaving the edges
of photographs or the smiles of family visitors
drinking tea beneath the clock.
As I snapped my head around I swear I could hear them,
drumming hooves inside old paperbacks,
speaking of lives I had almost lived,
mornings I knew that they had been,
had ridden over me, vanished into dawn
leaving palpable clues: unwashed cups in the sink,
a strange hair beside my pillow, a deep and frozen sadness
bitten like hoof prints into my brother's eyes.

Our Father, the Cartographer

After you had left us, had moved on from this world —
your spirit quiet as a knife in its sheath, blunt enough
to be drawn across the hand — after you had left us

only gargoyles grinning from roofs, pitchfork-wielding
gods, the fallen angel, had lured us sheer
to the rim of this cratered earth,

had eaten of our sorrow, spat its bones out,
even redrawn our very map of the world — networks of shadow
across the bed, your hand before the nightlight's light —

had warped our continents and distances, shrunken our ice caps,
swollen our oceans, leveled forests, washed out deserts,
diverted rivers, poisoned lakes and renamed countries

only to lay them back again to waste —

after you had truly come and gone,

had left us only shadows of your finery
deep in the dressing-up box of our skin, only then

could we know you as you really were, could we see
in your corpse the grandeur of the body,
broken now, and bloodied, shriveled down at last:

a tiny thing.

What Remains

Years later, driving us all
to rack and ruin in the blue Cortina, he would brake
suddenly, between Cheshire and Northumbria, listen
through glass for ghostly Roman legionaries
marching towards us over the frozen fields.
There would be no noise
for me but the wind, as usual: the strain of wire
strung out between wooden posts
along Dere Street.
Yet I did not want to think that he was crazy,
so I gripped my Tupperware sandwich box
full of Mr. Kipling's Almond Slices
and turned my head
to face the savage real:
a horned moon, minutes away
from setting, dark sheep
clustered like vagrants
in the shadow of a dry stone wall;
a snapshot of him
on leave from Egypt, riding his bike up the coast
with Dizzy Hill, Jock Ross and the lads
faking grown-up insouciance
with his cigarettes and Glenn Miller air —
a tribesman, perhaps, from a southern Roman colony,
paid gold to live away from home,
winding his legs with cloth to keep the snow out,

leaving behind
a single leather thong;
his idea of home
grown mirror-like and sentimental
as the shine on a pair of British Army boots —
symbolic of something vast
yet unimagined
which the tiniest act of rebellion
might cause to break —
a child, perhaps, twiddling her hair incessantly while
   he was driving —
her life called off, the troops pulled out
until all that remained of the progress of civilization
was a scale model of fortresses and ramparts; the unbroken relief of
barren land.

Flight

You have inherited his hands.
They stare back at you, slender-fingered,
pale as milk poured from a great height.

Hands that could have pushed him in right then
as you stood together over the languid river, watching pond-weed
hold its snake in check — fists startled by sunlight,
frozen an inch above his back

as, like a homing pigeon
you rose up from yourself to take the long view:
his imminent death, the strange collection of scars
with which he would leave you

shrunk back to the scabs of tractors, plough marks on a field
fifty feet below. The body you left beside him
ever watchful while your loose soul
grew to fit the sky.

Numb-fingered, how hard you try
even now, hunched like a jealous magpie over this keyboard,
to keep the urge to kill him gorgeous, distant:

a girl somewhere, her ailing father
stitched into the mist that now envelops her, its soft, grey cloth
polishing the bead of a songbird's eye.

Playing *Happy Families*

Laxatives turned gelid,
Three competing mirrors on a dresser,
An ancient, greying slice of hard-boiled egg:

Mr. and Mrs. Pitman both face down now
The sea's unwelcoming surface silent also
Overgrown, a self-unmaking bed

And nothing left of *Wor Jim* but these pieces
The Dot-dash here-and-gone of Souter Lighthouse
Warning ships off rock that once existed

A caricature
Dissolved into excuses
Fluttering down

Like butterflies, fuselage dust.

Cormorant

You do not need us to seem human.
Likewise the old pony that lives beside you grazing on fag ends,

The oozing symbols of its blinkered eyes.
Black dagger, oily with useless Tyne

No sentiment oozes out before you
The way it did when King Coal finally died,

Descendants of those who once mined this place
Now exhibited, in antique boots and blackface

At the Living Museum,
Employed to impersonate their fathers for minimum wage;

Grease-tinged boomerang
Dive deep without us, lend your name

To tankers, North Sea oil fields, tangle
In micro-filaments, shopping bags

While we become like brown rats in a drift mine
Skitter, scared, through coke dust, gnaw explosives —

The night is long. The lamps have all burnt down again.
Only the stones we walk on may survive.

The Idea of North

You say we are dead
We cannot exactly argue
Our silence deep, unagitated by diatoms
The spiraled sabers of narwhals, Arctic terns

Yet what remains of your quest but melted questions
Clocks frozen at the very instant of death
Ultima Thule picked clean, an inelegant sepsis
That suggests more than it says about what's lost:

Iodine, wind turbines
That photograph we took of you in profile
Needled, unencumbered and alert

A brief, quivering stasis of adventure
While, smeared across the crystal of ambition
We returned your gaze but did not grant permission
Failed natives of this blistered, ghost-wrecked place

Born in the Dark

Wild service, aromatic surgery, the sound of something evil born in the dark: as April showers splash into May we behave like plants of differing species, go back into spiritually violated literature, float silently in its scented pools, until the encounter finally loses its strangeness and all traces of dementia are eradicated: i.e. imagine the whole of Germany drenched in weird birdsong, brighter than these nitrate-enhanced fields.

ର

Your body burned, its ashes a modest teaspoon.
What shall we do next?
Leg bones the sizes of toothpicks continue to surface:
spring come so fast my lips flap in the wind of it—cherry
suicides, blue iris taunts.

C&

blue veins, asymmetric freckles, fine-grained vellum
white hairs, red hairs, black hairs amongst brown

slim green shoot, barrel of a tiny rifle
ice crack, stretch mark

rivered-through, deciduous, invulnerable
his or her haunches in the half light:

falling into, drowning past.

everything begins and ends in snow light:
soft mines, the mucus of despair,

this alphabet we crafted out of war wounds,
multiple and infinite,

clock black.

CR

milk work:
 suckled, answered:

milk work:
 :
unbroken, embodied:
 in no way
 and in no language
 what is said

Acknowledgements

Some of these poems have previously appeared, often in earlier versions, in the following publications: Grain, Event, The Malahat Review, SubTERRAIN, Canadian Woman Studies/les cahiers de la femme, Other Voices and Fireweed.

Thanks to the following, for their contributions to the development of this manuscript: Betsy Warland, Olga Broumas, Dionne Brand, Susan Leibik, Shauna Paull, Fiona Tinwei Lam. Thanks to everyone at Inanna, especially Luciana Ricciutelli. Thanks also to Wayne Hughes, Maggie Ziegler, Bronwen Merle, Lydia Kwa and everyone who attended the Sea to Sky poetry retreats, 2000 and 2001. And lastly, thanks to Dr. Adrianne Ross and the midwives of BC Women's Hospital.

The Heidegger quotation I use as my epigraph comes from his 1947 essay, "The Thinker as Poet."

The poem on page 16 is dedicated to the memory of Don Murray.

The poem cycle "Another Little Flower in God's Garden," beginning on page 66, concerns the notorious Moors Murders, carried out by Ian Brady and Myra Hindley in and around Greater Manchester in the mid-sixties. Some lines are taken from tapes Hindley and Brady made of the children before they were killed.

The poem on page 68 (part of the above cycle) takes its inspiration from the work of American poet Carolyn Forché, in particular The Angel of History.

Photo: Daniel Henshaw

Cathy Stonehouse is the author of a collection of short fiction, *Something About the Animal* (2011) and a previous collection of poetry, *The Words I Know* (1994). Co-editor of the creative non-fiction anthology *Double Lives: Writing and Motherhood* (2008), her poetry, fiction and nonfiction have appeared in a wide range of journals and anthologies including *White Ink: Poems on Mothers and Mothering* (2008) and *Beyond the Small Circle: Dropped Threads 3* (2005). Cathy emigrated to Canada from the UK in 1988 and currently lives in East Vancouver, where she writes, edits and teaches creative writing at various Lower Mainland colleges. Check out her website for more information: www.cathystonehouse.com.